RAILROAD

POSTCARDS

IN THE AGE

OF STEAM

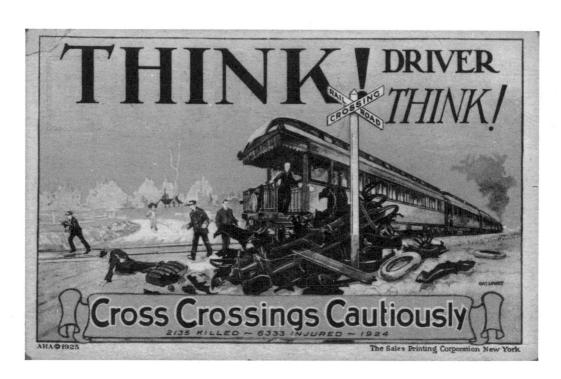

THINK! DRIVER THINK!

Cross Crossings Cautiously

2135 KILLED — 6333 INJURED — 1924

RAILROAD

H. Roger Grant

POSTCARDS

University of Iowa Press

IN THE AGE

Iowa City

OF STEAM

———

University of Iowa Press, Iowa City 52242

Copyright © 1994 by the University of Iowa Press

All rights reserved

Printed in the United States of America

Design by Richard Hendel

Printed on acid-free paper

Library of Congress Cataloging-in-Publication Data

Grant, H. Roger, 1943–

Railroad postcards in the age of steam / by H. Roger Grant.

p.   cm.

Includes bibliographical references.

ISBN 0-87745-465-5

1. Railroads—United States.   I. Title.

TF23.G67   1994

385′.0973′022—dc20   94-14552

CIP

01 00 99 98 97 96 95 94 C 5 4 3 2 1

for

KATHARINE BEERKLE DINSMORE

1876–1952

CONTENTS

ACKNOWLEDGMENTS

While the idea for a book on the picture postcard during the golden years of American railroading appealed to me, I did not develop it independently. John Vander Maas, who assembled the massive collection of view cards from which this album has been selected, and Paul Zimmer, director of the University of Iowa Press, encouraged me. Needless to say, I am indebted to both men.

I also received additional help. George Miller, professor of English at the University of Delaware and a leading authority on picture postcards, gave guidance. Boris Blick, a retired colleague from the University of Akron and a card collector, critiqued my essay. Similarly, George N. Johnson, Jr., a resident of Lexington, Virginia, and a postcard dealer, brought several important aspects of the postcard craze to my attention. And Robert A. McCown and the staff of the Special Collections Department at the University of Iowa Libraries handled effectively the copying of the cards from the Vander Maas collection.

Then there was my grandmother, Katharine Beerkle Dinsmore, who did much to stimulate my general interest in the past, including postcards. I vividly recall her large, green postcard album that contained wonderful views of midwestern places. Grandmother's cards from Hiteman, Iowa, a ghost town near my home community of Albia, especially intrigued me. This coal mining camp, which in 1910 sported a population of about 3,000 residents, was the location of my grandfather's drugstore. The sign on the false-front facade, "H. A. Dinsmore Drugs," captured on a real-photo card, made a lasting impression. Also memorable was the presence of the tiny Albia Interurban Railway in Hiteman. There were view cards of the modest interurban station and the company's several electric cars. That much-examined album also contained scenes of the coal miners' trains and the busy and multiple sites of the Wapello Coal Company, all of which fascinated me.

As with other books, my wife, Martha Farrington Grant, assisted me with this project. Although she is hardly a railroad enthusiast, she appreciates the picture postcards that once were so important to Americans.

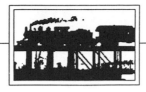

ABOUT THE POSTCARDS

When picture postcards initially appeared in the United States in the 1890s, collectors quickly emerged, and for the next two decades acquiring cards was the rage. Even though the craze faded by World War I, collecting continued, albeit with much less intensity. Collections, too, might be passed from one family member to another or simply stored. Then a major revival began in the 1970s. Thousands of enthusiasts, or deltiologists, reappeared, and they revitalized card-collecting groups. Dealers also entered the hobby; they found selling vintage images a lucrative activity.

This picture postcard excursion to the past was made possible by John P. Vander Maas, a retired Muscatine, Iowa, agribusinessman. He assembled a collection of approximately 27,000 railroad view cards and donated them in 1992 to the Special Collections Department of the University of Iowa Libraries in Iowa City. Although Vander Maas gathered cards from various sources, he acquired the vast majority from Arthur J. Petersen (1926–1989), a stamp and post-card dealer who lived near Madelia, Minnesota. The core of the Petersen holdings had come from a single source. Petersen purchased roughly a quarter of a million cards, accumulated in 440 shoe boxes, and subsequently sold many of the railroad ones to Vander Maas "at a good price." Since paper ephemera are often destroyed or damaged, the preservation and open access of these historic railroad cards have been a piece of good fortune.

RAILROAD

POSTCARDS

IN THE AGE

OF STEAM

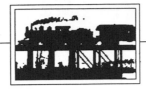

THE PICTURE POSTCARD PHENOMENON

Fads have repeatedly swept the United States. Whether the water-cure health phenomenon of the 1870s or crossword puzzles fifty years later, Americans seem utterly susceptible to various manias. One craze that burst upon the domestic scene in the early part of the twentieth century was the yearning for picture postcards. A writer for *American Illustrated Magazine* in 1906 appropriately called it "postal carditis." These small, attractive, and usually inexpensive printed pieces of durable paper were designed to be sent through the mail as a souvenir of a place or an event. Later they provided a convenient means for personal communication. Many of these cards, including posted ones, entered private collections, often bound smartly in portfolios that joined the family Bible and photograph album on the parlor table or at least in drawers with other cherished bric-a-brac. Collectors' clubs, too, sprang up.[1]

As is often the case with American fads, the origins of the postcard enthusiasm had foreign roots and preceded the zenith of public fascination. While there was no single inventor of the picture postcard, prototypes developed in Britain and elsewhere in Europe during the mid-nineteenth century. Pictorial mailing envelopes, for example, appeared in England during the 1840s, and Germans started to buy primitive view cards in the early 1870s. The introduction of the latter coincided with a growing movement in Europe and the United States for the postal card, namely an open piece of heavy paper of approximately three by five inches that required less postage than a regular letter. Much more aesthetically appealing view cards soon became the rage throughout much of Europe, except for Britain.[2]

Like the United Kingdom, the United States saw few examples of this genre because restrictive postal regulations discouraged the sale of privately printed picture postcards. When these items were offered, initially to celebrate the gala World's Columbian Exposition held in Chicago during 1893, illustrations might appear on drab government-issue postcards. Some of these "pioneer cards," however, were printed on better-quality stock, but the Post Office Department demanded two cents, double the rate of postage for regular cards.[3]

Those interested in picture postcards in the United States (and Britain, too) soon found it easier to participate in what had unmistakably evolved into a craze in countries like France, Germany, and Italy. A Magna Carta of sorts for these cards in America came on May 19, 1898, when Congress granted privately printed postcards the same postal rates as the government issues. Now a view card could go anywhere in the country for a penny.[4]

The removal of the remaining obstacle to the widespread use of these cards came on March 1, 1907. The Post Office Department decided that senders could legally write their messages on the *reverse* side. Before this ruling, which created the "split" or "divided" back with space for both address and message, it was common to find only limited blank margins on the front for a personal message. Specifically, the area where a very brief communication could be added measured a half inch or inch at the bottom or perhaps an inch or inch and a half on the right of the picture. The new format delighted enthusiasts; a picture card no longer needed to be defaced with handwriting, which sometimes meant a message scrolled across the picture itself.[5]

With the removal of annoying postal regulations, Americans could catch up with Europeans in their use of picture postcards. By 1907 they had a choice of several basic card types. A favored format and perhaps the most common were black-and-white cards (the vast majority of the album scenes belong to this category). While they might be printed domestically, they were typically products of German companies because of better price and overall excellence.[6]

Another popular form, the color view card, was also frequently printed in Germany from photographs supplied by American dealers. The German cards, superior in quality over the American, offered superb color with exceptionally sharp details. Although color photography was not yet commercially feasible, German producers converted black-and-white photographs into color by hand-coloring and a highly developed lithographic process. Actually, lithography had been invented in Germany in 1798, and by the late nineteenth century Germans had mastered this technically demanding art form. Even though the printing occurred thousands of miles away from the marketplace, these fancy German cards sold at prices competitive to those manufactured domestically. One drawback, however, was that the colors were not always correct. The customer might identify the color of various objects in the photograph, but a German card company employee made the final determination. Also, the maker might remove or add details to the photograph, thus at times considerably modifying the original image.[7]

The other option was the real-photo, or photograph, card. These picture postcards were exactly that: they were actual photographs printed on heavy postcard-size paper stock. The breakthrough came in 1902, when Eastman Kodak Company offered a special photographic paper on which images could be printed easily, effectively, and cheaply from negatives. Soon Kodak's rivals also entered what was evolving into a lucrative business, energized in part by that final liberalization of the postal code in 1907.[8]

The Kodak company further popularized the real-photo alternative with its introduction in 1903 of the Folding Pocket No. 3A, a special postcard camera. The photographer clicked the shutter and could open a special camera door and use a stylus to write a brief caption on the exposed postcard-size (3-1/4 by 5-1/2 inches) film. A contact print was then made on the appropriate paper stock for mailing.[9]

The popularity of picture postcards in the United States was impressive, even staggering, and extended nationwide. The Post Office Department reported the volume of postcards mailed during the twelve-month period that ended on June 30, 1908, at 667,777,798, and many were of the pictorial kind. The total for the same period five years later was nearly a billion. As a specific illustration of this extraordinary phenomenon, 18 million view cards were sold in Chicago during one month in 1907, and the estimated sales of cards nationally that year exceeded $50 million. When Congress debated tariff reform in 1909, which resulted in the Payne-Aldrich Tariff Act, anti-consumer protectionist lawmakers carried the day by placing a high ad valorem tax on foreign, namely German, cards. They believed that there was good reason to shelter domestic card makers: German producers were annually exporting literally tons of cards into the country to the detriment of American competitors.[10]

The immense popularity of postcards can be attributed to several factors. An obvious reason was the eye-catching, charming, and artistic quality of many cards. The pleasant distinctiveness of most foreign-produced cards and those from such domestic manufacturers as Detroit Publishing, Edward H. Mitchell, and Rotograph convinced even sophisticated consumers that they were acquiring something of beauty. Certainly, picture postcards of the pre–World War I era equaled or exceeded the attractiveness of the earlier trade cards, which were small advertising items, and much larger promotional posters.[11]

Unlike trade cards and posters, picture postcards were a boon to armchair travelers, who could collect the cards from places that they never really expected to visit. Although the older, hand-held stereopticon viewer, which required double-image view cards, had attractive features, picture postcards were cheaper and more plentiful. An Iowan, for example, who wished to see scenes of her grandparents' home community in Maine could acquire postcards, at least real-photo ones, from contacts in that faraway location. But stereopticon views were likely unavailable.[12]

In a related vein, picture postcards satisfied the public's desire for images, especially those depicting famous people and places. Newspapers and magazines offered scant competition. Only the wealthiest publishers could afford the halftone printing process that permitted direct reproduction of photographs. Early in the century they were used sparingly.[13]

Reasonable prices for picture postcards also enhanced sales. They were inexpensive, and most everyone, even children, could afford them. During the heyday of the infatuation, the retail price was usually a nickel for two cards. Commented one purchaser who mailed a card to his son in July 1910: "Hello Feedy! This card was only two and a half cents. . . . " At times consumers paid much less. A competitive marketplace, for instance, forced importers, jobbers, and retailers, who stockpiled cards from abroad in anticipation of the Payne-Aldrich Tariff Act of 1909, to slash their prices. A customer might pay as little as a nickel for ten cards before that overstock disappeared.[14]

A further explanation for the popularity of picture postcards includes more than their attractive features, ready availability, and reasonable costs; they could be used easily. Admittedly, the pre-1907 cards limited the opportunity to pen notes, but once the Post Office Department allowed space for messages on the back side, cards became miniletters. And that pleased the public. After all, people were usually in a hurry. "We as a nation are always moving, we are always in a hurry, we are never without momentum," concluded a magazine writer in

1908. Foreign visitors long before had commented that residents of the United States were constantly on the go. Americans even felt the need to be in motion when they relaxed, for the rocking chair was a popular piece of domestic furniture.[15]

As the habit of writing cards became more ingrained, social critics worried that the art of letter writing, never strong in the country, would be seriously threatened. George Finch, who contributed an essay on this subject to the June 1910 issue of the *American Magazine*, warned that there "arises a new danger which threatens even [the] . . . last citadel of letter writing, [love letters]." Infatuated couples could communicate speedily with each other, and that sparked postcard consumption. Finch observed that "the souvenir postal card courtship, if not an accomplished fact, is only a step in the future. Already a conversation a year long can be maintained at a cost of one cent per day in postage and from three to five cents in cards." He concluded in this somewhat tongue-in-cheek fashion: "No manufacturer has yet discerned any market for cards containing proposals in all forms and manners nor of answers in all degrees of enthusiasm. But the wise manufacturer will prepare, for, having furnished the material to lead a couple up to the crisis by the word of card, he must not desert them in their hour of need."[16]

The national postal service functioned well when these picture postcards were the rage. For one thing, the country benefited from the recently developed system of Rural Free Delivery. At a time when a large percentage of the population lived in the country (there were approximately 6.4 million farms in 1910), the direct delivery of mail to farmsteads greatly facilitated communication. Farmers traditionally ventured into towns only occasionally, perhaps on Saturdays if work schedules and weather permitted. On that day they shopped, gossiped, and picked up their mail at the post office. But with home delivery they could now read their cards and letters six days a week.[17]

Another factor leading to the rapid, dependable movement of the mails was the extensive network of steam and electric interurban railway lines. On the eve of World War I, the country boasted 254,251 route miles of the former and 15,580 route miles of the latter, near the peak mileage for both transport forms. Passenger and "fast mail" trains handled sealed, or "pouched," sacks of cards and letters, and the Railway Mail Service also staffed hundreds of specially designed and equipped Railway Post Office (RPO) cars on which en route sorting took place. In addition to this efficient rolling stock, RPO clerks were exceptionally productive. An explanation surely involved two elements: they received excellent wages, and they considered themselves to be among the elite of civil servants. This pride stemmed in part from their knowledge that they had done well on mandatory, periodic examinations that measured their speed and accuracy in the sorting process.[18]

The rapidity with which cards moved through the mails occurred not only because of the exceptional capability of the Railway Mail Service, "the Arteries of the Postal Service," but also owing to the common practice of "putting up" cards and letters in the private lock boxes of the smaller post offices after each delivery from the local depot and to the twice-daily (Monday through Friday) door-to-door delivery in larger communities. Some major cities witnessed even more frequent service in their commercial districts during the work week.[19]

The swiftness of mail delivery can easily be documented. Before about 1910, cards were postmarked twice, and that meant a date and time stamp was affixed at both the sending and receiving post offices. Thus it can be seen, for instance, how long it took a card to travel between the Indiana communities of Vincennes and Lewisville, 160 rail miles apart, on December 4, 1907. This particular card was posted by 9:00 A.M. in Vincennes and was stamped received at the Lewisville post office at 7:00 P.M. the same day. Although the card was carried on passenger trains of the Pennsylvania Railroad, it had to be transferred at Indianapolis; Vincennes and Lewisville were not on the same through line. An individual who lived in Vincennes or elsewhere within a radius of 100 miles or more might reasonably expect to receive a card sent on a Saturday that said "Come for dinner on Sunday" in time for the invitation to be meaningful.[20]

Even postcards that traveled great distances usually moved with dispatch. For example, a card mailed from Taunton, Massachusetts, on August 3, 1908, arrived in San Francisco four days later. One posted in 1912 from a rural Maine community reached London, England, within a week. A combination of fast passenger and mail trains and swift ocean liners helped to facilitate such remarkable surface movements.

In a related matter, whether assigned to a post office, a RPO car, or a country route, postal workers usually could deliver every piece of mail. They knew the geography, the unusual abbreviations, and the people in their communities. And they probably had learned to decipher most handwriting and to interpret creative spelling. This all occurred in an era when semi-literacy was common. "My patients would go on vacation and send postcards addressed to 'Dr. Bessie, New York City,' " recalled a former dentist who lived and worked in the Harlem section of the city, "and I would get those cards." This was not a rare testimonial.[21]

The high performance of the distribution process was fortunate since communication alternatives were limited or not considered practical. The nation's long-distance telephone network, which was just emerging, was unreliable and expensive. Moreover, many individuals could not call locally because they lacked telephones; there were only 82 telephones per 1,000 people in 1910 as compared to 280 per 1,000 in 1950. Access to telegraphic services was much better, but the public tended to use the offices of Western Union, Postal Telegraph, or the other companies only for emergencies, usually reporting a birth, illness, or death.[22]

When the multiple appeals of the picture postcards are considered, it is understandable why they were ubiquitous. Merchants of various kinds, especially druggists and stationers, carried them. Owners of specialized card shops also served customers in major cities. In the largest markets, cards were usually sold by retailers who relied on a chain of jobbers, importers, and printers. In the smallest markets, cards were less likely to have been mass produced. Rather than being the delicately colored views, they were more probably the real-photo variety. If they resembled cards found in urban and tourist areas, the seller had likely arranged with a printer to convert locally taken photographs into a small quantity of cards. Sometimes, too, a village retailer might carry a modest line of professionally produced greeting, special occasion, and comic postcards.[23]

The tens of millions of view cards sold during the time of national "postal carditis" covered a plethora of subjects. Scenes of public buildings, street-scapes, and natural wonders were in great demand. One popular category included views of various forms of contemporary transportation. While there were cards of automobiles, aircraft, trolley and interurban cars, steamboats, and ocean liners, railroad scenes dominated this genre. This was not unique to America. "Practically every country in the world with a railway line has produced at some time or other picture postcards featuring every aspect of the organisation from locomotives and rolling stock to views, from its stations to its staff and services," notes an authority on British railway cards. "The variety of cards produced almost defies the imagination; they have been produced in colour and black and white by chromolithography, collotype, and photography."[24]

The profusion of railroad cards in the United States coincided with the "Railway Age." Even though modal competition was dawning, most goods and people traveled on steel rather than on wooden or rubber wheels. Railroads were vital to American life, and their centrality was not lost on card makers. If consumers were in a city, they had choices of scenes of the union station or the large terminals of the individual roads. If they were in a village, it was the depot or the local railroad corridor that appeared on cards. Urban and country stations were public places and obvious subjects. Buyers likely considered these structures to be symbols of the community itself, as much or more so as government buildings, churches, or monuments.[25]

A good illustration of how the public perceived the railroad comes from St. Louis. The city's switching railroad, the Terminal Railroad Association of St. Louis, which the major carriers jointly owned, opened a splendid Romanesque-style union station in 1894. Its builder characterized the complex this way: "In this day the railway station is as much the means of entrance and exit to a city as was the bastioned gate of medieval times. It is therefore intended as a modern elaboration of the feudal gateway." St. Louisans agreed. "This lovely Union Station is our greatest building . . . [and] attests to the fact that this is the time of the modern railroad and the modern station," remarked a downtown businessman. "Visitors know that our Union Station is the gateway to the city and a *fine representation of it.*" Indeed, railway terminals mirrored civic pride and functioned as municipal showplaces.[26]

When the picture postcard fad struck St. Louis, visitors to Union Station and the city found a rich assortment of local views. However, there were more of the station available than of anything else, except in 1904 when scenes of the elaborate Louisiana Purchase Exhibition captured the public's fancy. When choosing a Union Station card, a customer might find two identical views, one taken in daylight and the other at night. At a glance that appeared to be the case. But, in fact, the printer had used the same negative for *both* cards. The trickster merely had darkened the sky, lighted the street lamps and the station windows, and added the moon.

This type of deception occurred widely. At times it was the result of photo pirating by publishers.[27]

While high quality German manufactured cards of St. Louis's Union Station predominated, it was also possible to purchase one of the real-photo variety. Actually, this card type was designed to focus attention not on the building but rather on the buyer. The district along Market Street, an east-west thoroughfare which passed on the north side of the main entrance of Union Station, and adjoining streets were studded with retail shops, and their owners, whether haberdashers, confectioners, or photographers, courted the traveling public. One such enterprise was Pruss Studios, which operated two stores convenient to the station. To exploit the picture postcard mania, the Pruss company and neighboring competitors photographed customers and quickly turned the negatives into real-photo cards. The subject might be placed in an open automobile with the ever-present backdrop of the station adorned with the signage, "Union Station St. Louis Mo." The front of the car might sport such smart sayings as: "Seeing St. Louis," "I am leaving St. Louis," "Hope to see you soon," or "We don't know where we're going, but we're on our way." Whatever the sign, the individual grasped the steering wheel, and if there were others, they sat alongside the presumed driver.[28]

In lesser places the choice of railroad picture postcards was more restricted; yet they were still available. The druggist, grocer, and perhaps the postmaster and depot agent sold them. In the smallest villages the cards were likely to be real-photo images. The limited market could not justify the expense of quality color cards or even ones printed in black and white, green on white, or sepia. The better cards, however, were usually available in larger communities, including county-seat towns.[29]

Regardless of the size of the community, a special event, where cards were needed quickly, resulted in the publication of real-photo images. It might be the arrival of an airplane, the visit of a national celebrity, a major conflagration, or the wreck of a speeding "flyer." Enterprising entrepreneurs immediately converted their photographs into cards and sold them, often in sets, in the local marketplace. When a Rock Island Railroad passenger train, operating over the tracks of the Chicago Great Western Railroad near Green Mountain, Iowa, derailed on March 10, 1910, killing fifty-five passengers and crew members, a photographer from nearby Marshalltown joined the relief train to the wreck site. Rather than aiding the surviving victims, he took scores of photographs of this awful and much publicized disaster. By the next day he peddled a packet of twelve cards that depicted the scenes of horror, including several exposed bodies along the right-of-way. Apparently his efforts were a financial success, for many of these cards have survived.[30]

Throughout the country the desire to carry a line of railroad cards was promoted by various factors. The profit motive was foremost. "I remember my dad [the agent for the Chicago, Milwaukee & St. Paul Railroad in Chatsworth, Iowa] always selling picture cards, thread, and other notions to travelers. It was a bother for his station work kept him hopping, especially when it was train-time . . . [but] the family always needed extra money. There must have been a good markup on these things." The cards, of course, were profitable to sell; an increase of 100 percent over cost or even more was common. And they were what people wanted. Buyers could pen on the front or back such appropriate remarks as "This is where we got off," "I took this train to town," "We rode in a car like this," and "Come and see me get off at this station."[31]

Making money, of course, does not fully explain the popularity of these ubiquitous cards. Many businesspeople believed that the fine cards of the local depot or railroad corridor represented good advertisement. Since the railroad was how outsiders reached their hometown, they wanted to convey that "live wires" and "go-getters" inhabited the place. Residents were enamored with the idea of progress, and for the community itself, progress meant growth, growth in population and real-estate values. Their motto was simply: "Don't Knock! Boost!" No wonder boosters relished the sight of a bulbous water tower with the town name emblazoned in six-foot-high letters. This explains why residents of the southwestern Iowa community of Stanton endorsed the signage on their water tower that proclaimed: YES—THIS IS STANTON. They could also buy a real-photo card of the tower with its spirited, large lettering. And railroad cards would help in a town's drive to become a second New York City, especially if the community sported a new brick depot, a nicely maintained "depot park," or impressive factories at trackside. Documenting that the settlement enjoyed rail service was an important first step toward a brighter future. When the Metropolitan Furniture Company of Springfield, Massachusetts, sought to promote both itself and the city about 1910, it distributed a complimentary card of the Springfield Union Station, an imposing brick and stone edifice. Such a selection was hardly startling; it fostered civic pride.[32]

Promoters who lacked suitable subjects like a union station could still use picture postcards effectively. Fakery occasionally occurred. One commercial photographer, who made real-photo cards of small midwestern towns, skillfully altered local scenes by adding to the negatives a street or interurban car and the necessary accoutrements of track and overhead trolley wire.[33]

Boosterism was hardly limited to residents of the nation's communities; railroad companies also aggressively promoted themselves. A better image presumably increased income. The larger carriers, in particular, had circulated trade cards during the late nineteenth century. The New York, Lake Erie & Western (Erie), for one, issued several types in the early 1880s that carried promotional statements or light verse on an illustrated cover and information about how to use the road on the back. They hoped that potential patrons grasped the significance of "TIME and the ERIE Wait for No Man" and:

CONCEIVE HIM IF YOU CAN,

AN ERIE R.R. YOUNG MAN.

WITH A SUIT OF BLUE CLOTHES,

BRASS BUTTONS IN ROWS.

A VERY POLITE YOUNG MAN.

Early in the twentieth century, steam and electric railroads began to distribute thousands of complimentary picture postcards from their city ticket offices, parlor cars, and other points of contact with the public. These cards featured attractions along their rights-of-way: parks, scenery, business opportunities, and the like. They also showed off corporate betterments of various sorts, including new pieces of motive power and state-of-the-art equipment. After all, postcard mania coincided with the second building of the country's railroads. Companies between the end of the depression of the 1890s and World War I spent hundreds of millions of dollars for new or replacement terminals, depots, bridges, "cut-off" lines, mammoth steam locomotives, and steel coaches. The strategy for the use of corporate-sponsored cards was summed up by the passenger traffic manager of the Chicago & North Western Railway in 1911, when he wrote: "We have found picture cards of our lines and equipment to be an excellent advertisement for the railway. . . . It gives credence to our 'Best of Everything' motto." His assessment was doubtlessly correct.[34]

Perhaps the most popular and surely the best remembered of the free railroad postcards were ones distributed by the Delaware, Lackawanna & Western Railroad (Lackawanna) before World War I. The focus was less on scenery and equipment and more on the road's image as a premier passenger carrier. The Lackawanna wished to publicize its attractive, safe, and "on-time" trains. Since company locomotives burned anthracite, or "stone," coal, passengers were not showered with much ash and soot as they traveled over a rehabilitated "speedway" between Hoboken, New Jersey (New York City), and Buffalo, New York. The railroad hired a New York advertising firm, Calkins and Holden, to develop the promotional campaign. The agency responded creatively; it produced a series of jingles that told of Miss Phoebe Snow, a beautiful young woman, like a Gibson girl, who wore white linen. Phoebe Snow was cool, comfortable, and unruffled. These rhyming advertisements appeared between 1900 and 1917 and were used in newspapers and magazines and on posters and postcards. Some of the most well liked were these:

> Says Phoebe Snow
> About to go
> Upon a trip
> To Buffalo:
> "My gown stays white
> From morn till night
> Upon the Road of Anthracite."

> Miss Snow draws near
> The cab to cheer
> The level-headed Engineer;
> Whose watchful sight
> Makes safe her flight
> Upon the Road of Anthracite.

Miss Snow commends
Her road to friends—
To one and all
This message sends:
"No route brings quite
As much delight
As cleanly Road of Anthracite."[35]

The smashing success of Phoebe Snow, which created much "Phoebeana," even caused a backlash. Competing roads, including the Erie and Lehigh Valley, were jealous and printed commentary that poked fun of her. In 1907, K. M. Chapman copyrighted and published in the form of a postcard a parody of the Phoebe Snow jingles:

A Phoebe Snow-drift

When Phoebe Snow went East one night
    Upon the Road of Anthracite,
She'd dined on lobster ere she left,
    And so of peaceful sleep bereft
She squirmed and tossed the whole night through,
    As restless sleepers always do,
And ere her "tummy" quit a hurtin',
    She'd poked her "tootsies" thro the curtain.
Then sweetest dreams came to her while
    Soft breezes fanned them in the aisle.

> Next morn the porter found them there
>> And tucked them in with zealous care;
> Said he, "I begs yo pardon, Miss.
>> De Lackawanna can't stand dis,
> We ain't objectin' to deir style,
>> You shore got Trilby beat a mile,
> But dem dat travels on dis line
>> Is jest de most perticler kine,
> An' throo de aisle dey'd 'fuse to go,
>> Blockaded by TWO FEET OF SNOW!"[36]

Apparently some risque Phoebe Snow parody cards also appeared. They were probably sold at the few shops, largely in urban centers, which pandered such items. Local governments, prodded by moral crusaders, repeatedly cracked down on these transactions, which violated municipal law and most citizens' sense of decency. The *New York Times* reported such a "bust" in 1905. Anthony Comstock, head of the Society for the Suppression of Vice, led two police officers, members of the "naughty picture squad," to a midtown New York stationery and novelty store after an employee had sold him several "improper" cards. Railroad postcards, however, generally had no interest for Comstock and others who fervently guarded public morals. Most images of the railway world were hardly controversial; indeed, they were considered good for the community.[37]

The deep-seated desire to boost, especially during the prolonged prosperity of the pre–World War I era, also found expression in a rich variety of railroad-related "gag," or comic, cards. One popular type cleverly overstated the special or superior quality of a particular place or regional product. Communities were certain of their greatness and eagerly sought to tell the world. This response resembled the later phenomenon of highway billboards proclaiming "The Friendliest Town in America," "The Flax Capital of the World," or "Where the West Begins."

Comic cards also reflected the humor of the day. Their creators, of course, stayed within the bounds of propriety; they did not want to attract the wrath of Anthony Comstock and his vice crusaders. An illustration of this card type is one published in about 1905, part of an Ohio "Whisperettes" series:

I wanted to go to Morrow, Ohio. I asked a man the quickest way to get to the depot. He said, RUN. When I reached the depot, there was a train on the side track:—I asked the agent, "Does this train go to Morrow?" He said, "No, it goes to-day." I told him I wanted to go to Morrow. He said, "Come down tomorrow and go." I told him I wanted to go to Morrow to-day. Just as the train was pulling out, I said, "IS THIS MY TRAIN?" He said, "No, it belongs to the R.R. Co." I said, "CAN I TAKE IT?" He said, "No, the R.R. Co. wants to use it." I went way back and sat down on a truck, telling the agent he was too fresh. He said, so was the paint on the truck.[38]

Other postcards of this kind exploited the public's common experience with railroads. Few Americans of the period lacked some firsthand ties with the railroad enterprise, and these cards attest graphically to the importance of railroads in their daily lives. Not surprisingly, creators of comic cards joined comedians from the vaudeville circuit and even songwriters to poke fun at individual carriers and aspects of life associated with the railroad enterprise. Typical of the humor that tapped the public's rich knowledge of railroading was the popular vaudeville wheeze, "I want to go to Chicago the worst way." "Take the Erie [Railroad]!" Composer Irving

Berlin also took a swipe at the "Weary Erie" when he wrote, "He may be as slow as the Erie," in his hit song "You'd Be Surprised."[39]

Although the picture postcard never disappeared, the craze had largely run its course by World War I. Multiple factors explain the fad's decline. Consumers by this time had another attractive choice: the modern greeting card, which included an envelope for a private message, gained in popularity. Indeed, like picture postcards, it was ideally suited for a population that did not enjoy composing long letters. Then there was the matter of the cards themselves. Since American-made view cards never equaled the excellence of the German ones, the outbreak of hostilities in Europe during the summer of 1914 seriously disrupted commercial ties between the Kaiser Reich and America. That trade had also been hindered earlier by the restrictive provisions of the Payne-Aldrich Tariff Act, although modifications had been part of tariff reform in 1913. While American manufacturers captured the domestic market, they turned out new cards that many collectors and perhaps the public found uninviting. View cards now commonly contained white borders; manufacturers wanted to save money by conserving ink. Previously, the best cards sported "full bleeds," that is, the image covered the entire front.[40]

Yet even before the war, Americans were tiring of picture cards. "I would estimate that 75 percent of the railroad cards that I have handled were mailed in the five-year period between 1907 and 1912," reflected a postcard dealer who specializes in railroad subjects. "The banner years seem to have been 1909 and 1910." That observation supports the comment made in a trade publication in 1913 that "the general condition of the post card business seems halfhearted." Fads fizzle, after all, and the picture postcard craze was no exception.[41]

The following album of railroad picture postcards represents a once-popular type of view card. It is divided into five sections and includes ones of locomotives and trains; railroad depots and related structures; the railroad corridor itself, with its tracks, bridges, and tunnels; people who were involved with railroading, either as employees, travelers, or casual observers; and comic and novelty cards. Most of these images date from the halcyon years of 1907 to 1912 and depict sites throughout the country.

The quality of the postcards in the album is consistently good. Additionally, the cards are aesthetically more appealing than later ones, including the "linens" that were popular during the 1930s and 1940s and the "chromes" that succeeded them. Fortunately, the zenith of railroading in American life corresponded with the production of German and real-photo cards. The latter effectively captured something that was transient. Argues one collector: "They really look like a real photograph of a building or train. . . . They also have that amateurish quality that gives them such authenticity." These postcards collectively not only provide a literal portrait of aspects of the railway age, they also reveal the flavor of a vanished past when railroads ably served a nation that witnessed pell-mell modernization.[42]

NOTES

1. John Walker Harrington, "Postal Carditis and Some Allied Manias," *American Illustrated Magazine* 61 (March 1906): 562–67; Julian Ralph, "Post-card Craze," *Cosmopolitan Magazine* 13 (October 1902): 97; George Miller and Dorothy Miller, *Picture Postcards in the United States, 1893–1918* (New York: Clarkson N. Potter, 1976), pp. 20–21; Sander Davidson, "Wish You Were Here," *American Heritage* 13 (October 1962): 97.

2. Frank Staff, *The Picture Postcard and Its Origins* (New York: Frederick A. Praeger, 1966), pp. 23–29, 44–63.

3. Miller and Miller, *Picture Postcards*, pp. 1–2.

4. Ibid., p. 2.

5. Ray D. Applegate, *Trolleys and Streetcars on American Picture Postcards* (New York: Dover, 1979), p. v.

6. Telephone interview with George N. John-

son, Jr., Lexington, Virginia, November 21, 1993, hereafter cited as Johnson interview, November 21, 1993.

7. Miller and Miller, *Picture Postcards*, pp. 16, 25, 27–28, 146.

8. Hal Morgan and Andreas Brown, *Prairie Fires and Paper Moons: The American Photographic Postcard, 1900–1920* (Boston: David R. Godine, 1981), pp. xiii–xiv.

9. Johnson interview, November 21, 1993; Morgan and Brown, *Prairie Fires*, p. xiv.

10. Miller and Miller, *Picture Postcards*, pp. 22, 26; *Nation* 89 (July 15, 1909): 51; *New York Times*, December 27, 1908.

11. Miller and Miller, *Picture Postcards*, pp. 149–57; telephone interview with George N. Johnson, Jr., Lexington, Virginia, September 23, 1993, hereafter cited as Johnson interview, September 23, 1993.

12. Johnson interview, November 21, 1993.

13. Frank Luther Mott, *American Journalism: A History of Newspapers in the United States through 260 Years: 1890–1950* (New York: Macmillan, 1950), pp. 588, 668; Frank Luther Mott, *A History of American Magazines, 1885–1905* (Cambridge: Harvard University Press, 1957), pp. 5, 153–54, 719–20.

14. Card in John P. Vander Maas collection, Special Collections Department, University of Iowa Libraries, Iowa City, hereafter cited as Vander Maas collection; Miller and Miller, *Picture Postcards*, p. 31.

15. Carlos A. Schwantes, *Railroad Signatures across the Pacific Northwest* (Seattle: University of Washington Press, 1993), p. 216; Arthur M. Schlesinger, "What Then Is the American, This New Man," *American Historical Review* 48 (January 1943): 225–44. Because postcards were open, unlike sealed letters, some correspondents sent their personal messages in code. See the album for an example.

16. George Finch, "Upon the Threatened Extinction of the Art of Letter Writing," *American Magazine* 70 (June 1910): 172–75.

17. *Historical Statistics of the United States: Colonial Times to 1957* (Washington, D.C.: U.S. Department of Commerce, 1960), p. 278.

18. Ibid., p. 429; George W. Hilton and John F. Due, *The Electric Interurban Railways in America* (Stanford, Calif.: Stanford University Press, 1960), p. 186; Bryant Alden Long and William Jefferson Dennis, *Mail by Rail: The Story of the Postal Transportation Service* (New York: Simmons-Boardman, 1951), pp. 1–80.

19. Long and Dennis, *Mail by Rail*, p. 2; interview with Louis W. Goodwin, Northfield, Connecticut, May 16, 1992, hereafter cited as Goodwin interview.

20. Johnson interview, September 23, 1993; *The Official Guide of the Railways* (New York: National Railway Publication Co., October 1908), pp. 469, 475.

21. Amy Hill Hearth, "Bessie and Sadie: The Delany Sisters Relive a Century," *Smithsonian* 24 (October 1993): 160.

22. John Brooks, *Telephone: The First 100 Years* (New York: Harper & Row, 1976), pp. 137–41; *Historical Statistics of the United States*, p. 480; Dan Knight to author, September 26, 1979.

23. Miller and Miller, *Picture Postcards*, pp. 16, 24, 146; Johnson interview, September 23, 1993.

24. William F. Rapp, "Railroad History via Post Cards: How We Got There," *Railway History Monograph: Research Journal of American Railways* 19 (July–October 1990): 2; Jeffrey Richards and John M. McKenzie, *The Railway Station: A Social History* (New York: Oxford University Press, 1986), p. 333; Maurice I. Bray, *Railway Picture Postcards* (Ashbourne, Derbyshire, England: Moorland Publishing, 1986), p. 9.

25. Richard Palmer and Harvey Roehl, *Railroads in Early Postcards: Volume One, Upstate New York* (Vestal, N.Y.: Vestal Press, 1989), p. v. See also John R. Stilgoe, *Metropolitan Corridor: Railroads and the American Scene* (New Haven, Conn.: Yale University Press, 1983).

26. *The St. Louis Union Station: A Monograph by the Architect and Officers of the Terminal Railroad Association of St. Louis* (Chicago: Bertram Allen Atwater, 1895), n.p.; *Globe-Democrat* (St. Louis), April 30, 1904.

27. Interview with Mark H. Cedeck, St. Louis, August 3, 1993.

28. Dante Carretti to "Memories," August 26, 1985, Memories Project papers, Barriger Collection, St. Louis Mercantile Library, St. Louis.

29. Goodwin interview.

30. H. Roger Grant, "The Green Mountain Train Wreck: An Iowa Railroad Tragedy," *Palimpsest* 65 (July–August 1984): 135–45.

31. "Autobiography of C. C. Searls," manuscript in possession of author; Goodwin interview.

32. H. Roger Grant and Charles W. Bohi, *The Country Railroad Station in America* (Sioux Falls, S.D.: Center for Western Studies, 1988), pp. 11–15. The Metropolitan Furniture Company card is found in the album.

33. Johnson interview, November 21, 1993. See also John W. Ripley, "The Art of Postcard Fakery," *Kansas Historical Quarterly* 38 (Summer 1972): 129–31.

34. Albro Martin, *Railroads Triumphant: The Growth, Rejection and Rebirth of a Vital American*

Force (New York: Oxford University Press, 1992), pp. 110–32; John E. Merriken, *Every Hour on the Hour: A Chronicle of the Washington, Baltimore & Annapolis Electric Railroad* (Chicago: CERA Bulletin 130, 1993); A. C. Johnson to Marvin Hughitt, February 25, 1911, Chicago & North Western Railway Company papers, Chicago & North Western Transportation Co., Chicago.

35. Rodney O. Davis, "Earnest Elmo Calkins and Phoebe Snow," *Railroad History* 163 (Autumn 1990): 88–92; Robert J. Casey and W. A. S. Douglas, *The Lackawanna Story: The First Hundred Years of the Delaware, Lackawanna and Western Railroad* (New York: McGraw-Hill, 1951), pp. 173–83.

36. Seth M. Bramson, "Phoebeana," *Railroad History* 165 (Autumn 1991): 114–16.

37. *New York Times*, October 28, 1905.

38. Card in Vander Maas collection.

39. William Pickett Helm, "You Got Another Papa on the Erie Line," *Collier's* 84 (December 28, 1929): 12.

40. Miller and Miller, *Picture Postcards*, pp. 26, 32; telephone interview with George N. Johnson, Jr., Lexington, Virginia, November 7, 1993, hereafter cited as Johnson interview, November 7, 1993.

41. Johnson interview, November 7, 1993; Miller and Miller, *Picture Postcards*, p. 32.

42. Johnson interview, September 23, 1993.

TRAINS AND ROLLING STOCK

*Heavy snows repeatedly disrupted railroad operations. While this card dates from 1906,
it looks back to a scene on the New York, New Haven & Hartford Railroad during the famed
"Blizzard of 1888," which caused extensive loss of life and property destruction.*

First Train to arrive in South Norwalk, Conn, after the Blizzard of 1888.

4-2-06
GRACE M. SNYDER,
SEYMOUR ST.,
So. NORWALK, CT.

Many thanks for your lovely card. This ?? Blizzard
was March 12-14. We very near had another this March 19-06

"Winter Railroading" at Ishpeming, Michigan, in the state's Upper Peninsula, dates from 1912 and shows two snow-covered locomotives that are likely from the Chicago & North Western Railway.

Winter Railroading, Ishpeming, Mich.

The Green Bay & Western Railroad, which operated a trans-Wisconsin route,
regularly battled the elements, including the effects of an ice jam on the Wisconsin River
in the spring of 1906.

GREETINGS FROM GRAND RAPIDS WISCONSIN

A. P. Hirzy, Pub.

ICE JAM IN WISCONSIN RIVER, AT G. B. & W. R. R. BRIDGE, APRIL 7, '06.

When snow reached great depths, railroads turned to the mighty rotary plow, if they owned or could borrow one. A hardy photographer caught a train fighting drifts near Estherville, Iowa, on either the Minneapolis & St. Louis or the Rock Island Railroad in February 1909.

GREETINGS FROM ESTHERVILLE, IOWA.

THE ROTARY STEAM SNOW SHOVEL AT WORK
FEBRUARY–1909.

The time of intense postcard interest coincided with the introduction on several railroads of powerful, yet slow-moving Mallet compound steam locomotives. Essentially two engines under a single boiler, a Mallet's rear high-pressure engine was rigidly attached to the locomotive frame, while the front low-pressure engine pivoted so that it could swing independently of the rest of the locomotive.

An unusually long freight train rolls past a photographer at an unidentified location early in the century. Freight trains were much less likely to appear on picture postcards than were more glamorous passenger trains.

The everyday task of switching is taking place in the freight yards of the New York,

Chicago & St. Louis Railroad, the "Nickel Plate Road," in the north-central Ohio community of

Bellevue in about 1910.

A cabbage-stack Shay-geared locomotive, owned by a private lumber company, waits to pull a cut of cars loaded with pine logs near Bogalusa, Louisiana. It is headed for a connection with the New Orleans Great Northern Railroad.

Bales of cotton fill a gondola car in Memphis, Tennessee. This staged photograph was surely intended to promote the city's image as a principal cotton market.

A special freight train on the Southern Pacific Railroad prepares to leave the Imperial Valley of California with a remarkable load of cantaloupes. The large size of the card is appropriate for this subject.

World's Record Cantaloupe Tr
JUNE 21ST 1908 ✻ 89 Pacific Fruit Express Re
SOUTHERN PACIFIC CO. in ONE SOLID TRAIN
or approximately 1,557,500 cantaloupes
ONE-DAY'S OUTPUT from IMPERIAL VALLEY

...in FROM IMPERIAL VALLEY
...frigerator Cars, handled by the
...containing 31,150 CRATES
...onsigned to Eastern markets
Total Weight 3,560 Tons.

Copyrighted 1908
A.P.Center

The management of the St. Paul and Tacoma Lumber Company must have taken considerable pride in this promotional view of an enormous chunk of Douglas fir. The card is typical of many of the times in that it is "Made in Germany" and it prominently displays the name of the importer and publisher.

"A. Washington Fir."

A few minutes after train-time at the massive St. Louis Union Station, a crack passenger train moves into the yards and exits from a city that rightly called itself "The Railroad Crossroads of America."

Passenger Train Leaving Union Station. St. Louis, Mo.

One of the South's premier passenger carriers, the Louisville & Nashville Railroad operated a popular travel route between Cincinnati and New Orleans. A passenger train races over a bridge across a bayou near the Gulf of Mexico.

L. & N. Train Crossing Bridge, Ocean Springs, Miss.

Although this card was mailed in 1908 and has a split back, the correspondent still

penned commentary on the front. A mainline Wabash Railroad passenger train pauses at

Mexico, Missouri, a busy county-seat community in the central part of the state.

164. Wabash Depot, Mexico, Mo.

C. U. WILLIAMS, PHOTOETTE, BLOOMINGTON, ILL.

It's train-time at Burlington Junction, Missouri, a small railroad-created community

on the Wabash Railroad's Omaha line and the Burlington Route's Nodaway Valley branch.

A crowd gathers at the Santa Fe station in San Diego, California, in about 1910. This card, published by the Edward H. Mitchell Company of San Francisco, represents one of the quality American-made images.

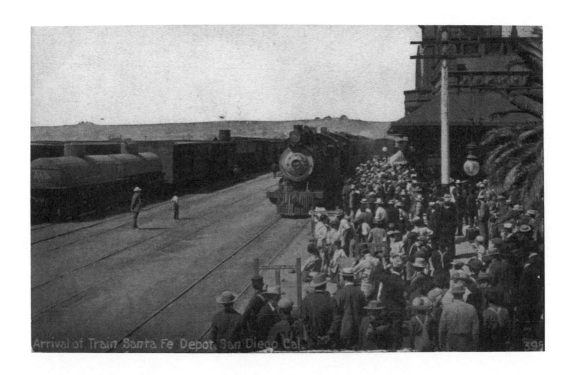

Arrival of Train Santa Fe Depot, San Diego Cal.

A passenger train on the Colorado Springs & Cripple Creek District Railway blasts up a grade west of Colorado Springs, Colorado, in 1909. This particular view card was distributed to conventioneers in Denver by the Rocky Mountain News *and the* Denver Times.

St. Peter's Dome.—On Cripple Creek Short Line.

In an obviously staged scene, two narrow-gauge passenger trains of the Colorado &
Southern Lines travel around the famed "Loop" near Georgetown, Colorado. This image was
printed by the Detroit Publishing Company, a pioneer producer of fine view cards.

A Southern Pacific Lines passenger train passes over the magnificent Pecos River bridge in West Texas. This spindly structure opened in 1892 and was replaced with a more substantial one in 1944.

"PECOS RIVER BRIDGE"
LENGTH: 1516 FEET
HEIGHT: 321 FEET
WEIGHT: 7,124,000 LBS.
HL.© COMPLETED: MARCH 1892

The Atlantic & West Point Railroad and the Western Railway of Alabama, which jointly operated between Atlanta, Georgia, and Selma, Alabama, formed part of the "Great Trunk Line between the North and South." This arrangement was a link in a through line between New York and New Orleans that also included the Pennsylvania, Southern, and Louisville & Nashville railroads. The complimentary promotional card attests to the superb dining facilities offered by the "West Point Route" on its best trains.

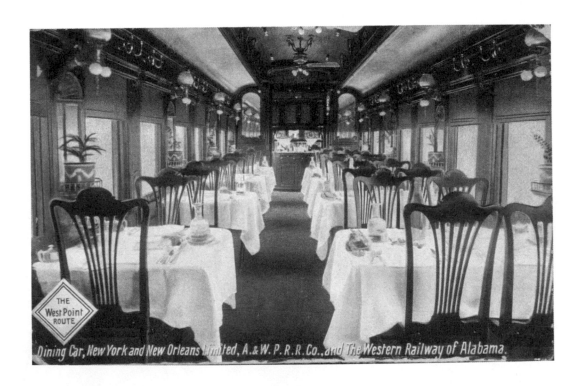

Dining Car, New York and New Orleans Limited, A. & W. P. R. R. Co., and The Western Railway of Alabama.

THE
West Point
ROUTE

Not until the appearance of the Zephyrs *in the 1930s did the Chicago, Burlington & Quincy (Burlington Route) become a leading passenger-carrying road. Yet the company provided several attractive name-trains earlier in the century. The road never operated the "Burlington Limited"; it was simply a generic name for its better "varnish." The view of the dining car appeared on a card specifically designed for attendees "Enroute to Chi Omega Fraternity Convention, Boulder, Colorado" in 1914.*

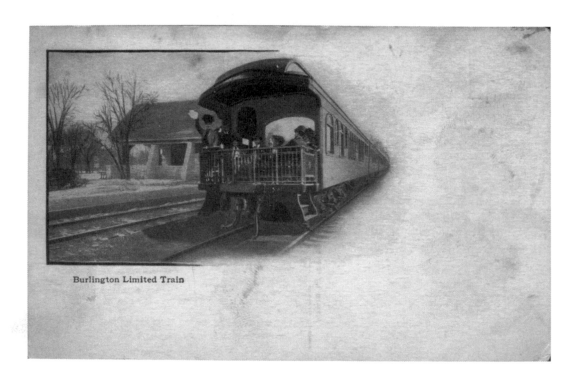

Burlington Limited Train

James J. Hill's Great Northern Railway, a modern speedway between Minneapolis-St. Paul and Seattle, offered passengers after 1905 splendid accommodations on board its Oriental Limited. *It was truly "The Perfect Train to Puget Sound."*

AFTERNOON TEA ON THE ORIENTAL
LIMITED, GREAT NORTHERN
RAILWAY. SEE AMERICA FIRST.

Typical during the time of real-photo cards, an aggressive photographer captured a wreck scene.
These "Clearing Up the Soo Wreck" cards were likely part of a set of views taken of a freight-train
mishap near Superior, Wisconsin.

Clearing up the Soo Wreck
Superior, Wis.

Special tourist lines flourished during the age of steam. Rather than carrying both "hogs and humans," these roads handled only the latter. The Mount Washington Railroad hauled sightseers from Bretton Woods, New Hampshire, to the top of Mount Washington. "Only Yankees," the joke went, "would build a cog railway so that they could enjoy the worst weather in New England." Less breathtaking was the scenery along the nine-mile Mammoth Cave Railroad. This tourist pike linked Glasgow Junction, Kentucky, a connection with the Louisville & Nashville Railroad, with the subterranean delights of Mammoth Cave.

ARRIVAL AT THE SUMMIT, MT. WASHINGTON, N.H.

Mammoth Cave Dinkey

Wrecks, unfortunately, have always been part of railroading. With better rolling stock, mandated by the federal government's Safety Appliance Act of 1893, the numbers of accidents diminished somewhat, but they continued to occur. In this postcard scene, taken in April 1909, boxcars on a Delaware & Hudson Railroad freight train somehow left the rails in Sidney, New York.

D. & H. Wreck, Sidney (N. Y.) yard April 4th. 1909

Amusement park operations were the rage after the turn of the century. One of the more popular was operated by a religious commune, the House of David, in Benton Harbor, Michigan. This sect also was famous for its baseball team that barnstormed throughout the Midwest, creating a sensation because of the players' long beards.

House of David Park

DEPOTS

AND

RAILWAY

STRUCTURES

Residents of Springfield, Massachusetts, had reason to be proud of their Romanesque-style union station. This architecturally significant structure was created by Shepley, Rutan, and Coolidge, a leading design firm. The edifice opened in 1889, and by the 1900s it served trains of the Boston & Albany, Boston & Maine, Central New England, and New York, New Haven & Hartford railroads.

No. 10 Railway Station, Springfield, Mass.

COMPLIMENTS OF

METROPOLITAN FURNITURE CO.

SPRINGFIELD, MASS.

The college and industrial town of Northampton, Massachusetts, had a union station that was used by both the Boston & Albany and New Haven railroads. Its exceptionally long platform cover gives it a distinctive appearance.

Railroad Station.   Northampton, Mass.

While the card maker identified the depot at Delano, Pennsylvania, as being a Lehigh Valley Railroad facility, it was actually a union station. The Pennsylvania Railroad also served it.

L. V. R. R. Station, Delano, Pa.

12862

The predecessor of the Grand Central Station in New York City was an imposing structure. Yet it could not accommodate adequately the growing volume of traffic on the New York Central and New Haven railroads early in the century. Therefore, it was replaced by the "World's Greatest Railway Terminal," Grand Central Station, in 1913.

GRAND CENTRAL DEPOT N.Y.

PUBL. BY ILL. POST. CARD CO., NEW YORK

Surely the best-known urban railroad terminal in the United States was the Pennsylvania Railroad Station in New York City. This building, designed by the famous firm of McKim, Meade, and White, opened in 1910 and served the traveling public until the 1960s. Some students of Gotham have argued that Penn Station was as much a symbol of the city as the later Chrysler and Empire State buildings.

213

PENNSYLVANIA RAILROAD STATION, NEW YORK.

Better known as the Pennsylvania Railroad Station because only the Pennsylvania and its affiliated roads used it, this imposing structure began serving Pittsburgh in 1901. The architect was the gifted D. H. Burnham. The spelling of Pittsburg is not a misprint; rather, the city had dropped the "h" during this time.

Union Station, Pittsburg, Pa.

Detroit Union Depot, designed by Isaac S. Taylor, dates from 1889. By 1910 trains of the Canadian Pacific, Detroit, Toledo & Ironton, Pere Marquette, and Wabash railroads used this facility.

Union Depot. Detroit, Mich.

These interior views of St. Louis Union Station, the handiwork of architect Theodore C. Link, show the Midway, which connected the headhouse and the trainshed, and the Grand Hall on the Market Street level. The facility opened on September 1, 1894.

Midway, Union Station. St. Louis, Mo.

271 Grand Hall, Union Station, St. Louis.

Oklahoma City, the bustling capital of the new state of Oklahoma, lacked a true union station early in the century. Yet the Frisco and Rock Island railroads shared this facility before the 1930s. The city's other major railroads, Missouri, Kansas and Texas (Katy), and Santa Fe, served travelers elsewhere.

The sender of this picture postcard of the Southern Railway's station in New Orleans missed the mark when he wrote, "One of two Union Depots of New Orleans, La." The city actually had four separate stations. This terminal facility, which handled trains of both the Frisco and Southern railroads, opened in 1908, the design work of D. H. Burnham and Company.

One of the two Union Depots of New Orleans, La.

The small Indiana city of Vincennes could claim a union station. This facility was a stop for trains on the Baltimore & Ohio, Chicago & Eastern Illinois, and Pennsylvania railroads. It also included hotel rooms, a service not unknown in America. The comment on the bottom of the card is typical of the era: "Come and see me get off at this station."

While hardly a metropolis, Hoopeston, Illinois, could tell the world on a picture postcard

that it, too, sported a "union depot." Trains of the Chicago & Eastern Illinois and the Lake Erie

& Western railroads paid daily calls. Railroads usually preferred union stations rather than

separate ones; they could significantly cut their local operating costs.

The Wabash Railroad provided the principal service in the north-central Missouri county-seat town of Moberly. Yet the community had a union station; Hannibal division trains on the Katy Railway also served the depot.

Union Station. Moberly, Mo.

Guess you are happy with Granny this morning. Write to me soon — Mary —

Residents of Le Mars, Iowa, were surely proud of the station shared by the Chicago, St. Paul, Minneapolis and Omaha (Omaha) and Illinois Central railroads. The Omaha had trackage rights over the Illinois Central from Le Mars to Sioux City, Iowa, a distance of twenty-five miles.

An affiliate of the Southern Pacific Railroad, the "Sunset Route" owned this Spanish-mission-style station in San Antonio, Texas. It remains in service today to accommodate several Amtrak trains.

A train with a snowplow attracts onlookers at the Boston & Maine Railroad station at Danbury, New Hampshire. The two-story depot provided living quarters for the agent and the agent's family in this small New England community.

A crowd poses for the camera next to the Lehigh Valley's frame, combination

depot in Berkshire, New York. The building was the community's portal to the outside world.

Lehigh Valley R.R. Station, Berkshire, N.Y.

A passenger train of the Grand Rapids & Indiana Railway, the "Fishing Line," part of the Pennsylvania Railroad system, steams into the station at Plainwell, Michigan, a village between Kalamazoo and Grand Rapids.

The Chicago, Burlington & Quincy Railroad typically constructed combination depots with wide eaves throughout its midwestern service territory, including ones at Abingdon and Zearing, Illinois.

Zearing, Ill.

ZEARING.

Dunham Photo
Princeton, Ill.

The Chicago, Burlington & Northern, a component of the Chicago, Burlington & Quincy, built this distinctive depot at Bagley, Wisconsin, from a standardized plan. It is nearly train-time in this 1908 view.

The Rock Island Railroad gave Indianola, Iowa, a county-seat town in central Iowa and home of Simpson College, a Methodist institution of higher education, an attractive brick, stucco, and tile depot. The community, however, was merely at the stub end of a branch from Des Moines.

Schuster Studio of Hermann, Missouri, created this "Sectional View of Hermann, Mo.,"
which features in the foreground the wooden combination depot of the Missouri Pacific Railway.

S. 106   Sectional View of Hermann, Mo.   SCHUSTER STUDIO
                                                                            HERMANN, MO.

A crowd gathers in about 1920 at the stone Missouri Pacific depot in Warrensburg, Missouri, a county-seat and college town. Central Missouri State Normal, today's Central Missouri State University, generated passenger business for the railroad.

The Katy Railway depot at Dewey, Oklahoma, reflects the company's architectural taste in small-town station structures.

Colorado in 1910 claimed three railroad stations with the name "Summit." This view card shows Summit, Teller County, on the mountainous line of the Colorado Springs & Cripple Creek District Railway. The other Summits were in El Paso and San Juan counties.

"The New Depot" is part of the caption placed by the printer on this view of the station of the Denver & Rio Grande Railroad at Palisade, Colorado, near Grand Junction. A previous building had likely burned.

The New Depot, Palisade, Colo.

The Great Northern Railway had recently completed this brick depot at

Havre, Montana, a railroad division center, college town, and important shipping point.

Great Northern Depot, Havre, Mont.

While hardly a depot, either the Katy Railway or a private entrepreneur erected the "Katy Hotel," in Katy, Texas, a creation of the railroad twenty-eight miles north of Houston.

The station complex at Sparks, Nevada, includes the dispatchers' office. This facility

made possible the control of Southern Pacific trains across desolate sections of the Sagebrush state.

The Railroad "Y" movement of the Young Men's Christian Association (Y.M.C.A.), which started in Cleveland, Ohio, in 1872, operated nearly two hundred of these specialized Y.M.C.A.'s by World War I. One was designed for employees of the Gulf, Colorado & Santa Fe (Santa Fe), Katy, and Trinity & Brazos Valley railroads in Cleburne, Texas.

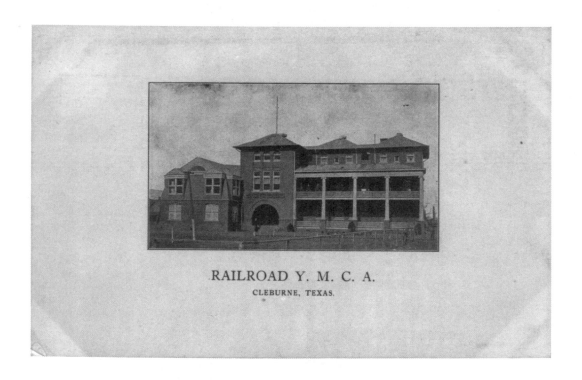

RAILROAD Y. M. C. A.

CLEBURNE, TEXAS.

A collage of scenes from Kempton, Ford County, Illinois, predictably includes a view of the depot. The village of 269 residents was proud of its Illinois Central Railroad station.

When a combination depot was inadequate for the freight needs of a community, railroads erected separate freight houses like this one built by the Great Northern Railway in Minot, North Dakota.

G. N. FREIGHT HOUSE MINOT N. D.

Railroad companies commonly rented quarters in buildings to serve as ticket offices. Some, including the Great Northern Railway, even maintained space to promote their service region. The Great Northern's Information Bureau once stood near the union station in St. Paul, Minnesota.

Great Northern Railway Free Information Bureau and Exhibit Rooms, St. Paul. Two doors from Union Depot. Stop over on your way West and see this display of grains, grasses and fruit from the Great Northwest.

Where the "Nickel Plate Road" crossed the Cincinnati, Hamilton & Dayton Railway

in Leipsic Junction, Ohio, the two carriers shared a combination depot and tower complex.

This union station of sorts was mostly for train-control work.

LEIPSIC JUNCTION. LOOKING WEST ON NICKLE PLATE R.R.   LEIPSIC O.

Much less impressive than most towers is this unknown one, probably

on a rural rail line. The "GF" sign is the facility's telegraphic code identification.

One of the smallest and most mundane of American railway structures was the road-crossing guard's shanty. Railroad companies frequently assigned elderly or injured employees to these boring and low-paying jobs.

A common railroad structure was the roundhouse, or engine shed. Although not a full circle, the roundhouse of the Santa Fe Railway at Waynoka, Oklahoma, was nevertheless a sizable building.

A.T.&S.F. ROUNDHOUSE.   WAYNOKA-OKLA.

The sender of the view card of the Pennsylvania Railroad suburban station at Wildwood, New Jersey, near Philadelphia, decided to add his own art work. In the scene of the Iowa Central depot at Ackley, Iowa, the publisher wished to make certain that everyone knew the card's place of origin. The signboard is hardly what actually adorned the building.

Penna. R.R. Station, Wildwood, N.

Iowa Central Depot, Ackley, Iowa.

ACKLEY

THE

RAILROAD

CORRIDOR

A train of the Boston & Maine Railroad has passed through a scenic cut near Newbury, New Hampshire, in 1907.

„Train in Cut" near Lake Sunapee, Newbury, N. H.

July 27 to Aug 1st, 1907

33184 Pub. by J. H. Johnson, Bradford, N. H. Germany

The mountainous terrain of the Southern Tier of New York is readily

apparent in this view of the mainline of the Erie Railroad near Lordville, New York.

Published By George V. Millar & Co., Scranton, Pa, 4638 L

CURVE ABOVE LORDVILLE, N. Y.

The right-of-way of Henry Flagler's "Overseas" extension is being readied for track at Long Key, Florida, in about 1911. Known as "Flagler's Folly," this Florida East Coast Railway line between Knights Key and Key West opened in January 1912.

32 THE RIGHT OF WAY AND MEN'S QUARTERS ON LONG KEY, FLA. F. E. C. RY. EXTENSION SERIES

Likely the most famous section of right-of-way in the country is Horseshoe

Curve, on the mainline of the Pennsylvania Railroad west of Altoona, Pennsylvania.

A 20301   Horseshoe Curve, Allegheny Mts. - Pennsylvania Railroad.

are not ch
for me, r

*I have mislaid your
Hbg. address, when you
... put itt on a card
... you?
Sincerely
N. K. m*

There are horseshoe curves far less impressive than the one near Altoona, Pennsylvania. One was once near Waukon, Iowa, on the Chicago, Milwaukee & St. Paul's twenty-three-mile Waukon Junction–Waukon branch.

Horse Shoe Curve, Iron Mine Route, Waukon, Iowa.

A train on the Illinois Central Railroad charges past
"Sentinel Rock" near Dawson, Kentucky, in about 1906.

While the Quanah, Acme & Pacific Railway never reached the Pacific Ocean, it did connect the Texas communities of Quanah and Floydada, a distance of 111 miles. The road cut through the caprock escarpment when it built an extension between MacBain and Floydada in the late 1920s.

The Line of the Quanah, Acme & Pacific Railway approaching the Staked Plains of West Texas Near Dougherty, Texas

The Uintah Railroad, a spectacular thirty-six-inch-gauge railroad that extended from Mack, Colorado, to Watson, Utah, served Gilsonite (asphalt) mines near Dragon, Utah, and was one of the world's most crooked lines. One stretch of twelve miles contained 233 curves and bends. A view card shows Baxter Pass, which sported grades of 7-1/2 to 8 percent. This shortline opened in 1904 and closed thirty-five years later.

UINTAH RY. 7½ % GRADE

A later affiliate of the Union Pacific Railroad, the Saratoga & Encampment Railroad operated over a forty-four-mile line between the Wyoming communities of Walcott and Encampment in the southeastern part of the Equality state.

Scene on S. & E. R. R., 5 miles from Encampment, Wyo. Fine Fishing Here.

—Lordier Drug Company

Part of the metropolitan corridor is the ever present rail yard. The Queen & Crescent

Route's major yards in Meridian, Mississippi, are captured in this ca. 1910 picture postcard.

The station, support facilities, and yards of the Burlington Route in

Beatrice, Nebraska, were partially flooded when this real-photo card was made in 1911.

This "birdseye" real-photo card catches the railroad facilities and commercial and residential sections of a raw Gillette, Wyoming, a town created by the Burlington Route in the state's northeastern section.

The waterfront rail facilities of the Southern Pacific Railroad in

San Pedro, California, the port for Los Angeles, are shown in this ca. 1910 image.

Where Water & Rail Meet, Los Angeles Harbor, San Pedro, Cal. 703

A vital part of the railroad corridor is the bridge. This Pennsylvania Railroad stone arch structure at Rockville, Pennsylvania, immediately north of Harrisburg, crosses a wide Susquehanna River.

P. R. R. BRIDGE, ROCKVILLE, PA. THE LONGEST STONE ARCH BRIDGE IN THE WORLD

The sender of this picture postcard of a deck and truss bridge on the Tallulah Falls Railway in Georgia explains the scene: "This view shows the little 'Dinkey' which conveys people out to Tallulah Lodge, and the man who runs it is called the Dinkey man." The fifty-seven-mile shortline connected the communities of Cornelia, Georgia, and Franklin, North Carolina.

A Pere Marquette Railroad passenger train rumbles over a long trestle that spans
Michigan's Sauble River. The writer asks on the left-hand margin: "Are you collecting Post-Cards,"
a not-so-unusual query.

R.R. Trestle
Over
Sauble River.

The "Bridge and Train Scene, Forest City, Iowa" finds an Iowa Central Railway passenger train atop the Winnebago River bridge near this northern Iowa community. The card, like so many of the day, was posted on a Railway Post Office (RPO) car, "Tr. 3, St. Paul & Des M, August 27, 1909."

BRIDGE AND TRAIN SCENE, FOREST CITY, IOWA.
PINCKNEY BROS., DRUGGISTS

While Anderson Mill in Anamosa, Iowa, is mostly concealed by foliage, a railroad bridge, with its many deck bents, dominates the scene.

THE ANDERSON MILL   ANAMOSA IOWA.   NOH.

The railroad bridge of the Spokane, Portland & Seattle Railway parallels a wagon bridge near Camas, Washington, twenty-four miles east of Portland, Oregon.

No 8. S.P.+S.RR., AND WAGON BRIDGES, CAMAS, WASHINGTON.

The rugged country traversed by the Alaska Railroad is seen

in this view of the extensive trestle work over the Bartlett Glacier.

BARTLETT GLACIER-
AND HIGH TRESTLE GOV. RY. MILE 49 ALASKA

A crowd greets a Denver & Salt Lake Railway train at the
west portal of the 6.2-mile Moffat Tunnel, about 50 miles west of Denver.

15713. West Portal, Moffat Tunnel, Colo.

The location of this real-photo scene is unknown, but the image is typical of the ever-changing environment in timber country.

Forest products have long moved by rail. A sawmill operation in the Black Hills of South Dakota, with its private industrial railroad, is shown on this 1909 real-photo card.

Coal, like lumber, traveled mostly by rail during the early twentieth century, and coal-carrying roads, especially the anthracite ones, prospered. The Bellevue Breaker (for coal sorting) adjoins the tracks of the Delaware, Lackawanna & Western, the "Road of Anthracite," in northeastern Pennsylvania.

1773 Bellevue Breaker, Scranton, Pa.   J. D. Williams & Bro. Co., Publishers.

The coal docks for loading cars on the Wheeling & Lake Erie Railway at Dillonvale, Ohio, near Steubenville, are part of the blighted landscape of southeastern Ohio.

The Duluth, Missabe & Northern Railway, one of the world's great

haulers of iron ore, serves mines on its Wilpen branch at Chisholm, Minnesota.

Chisholm and Clark Mines, Chisholm, Minn.

A gondola car of the Buffalo & Susquehanna Railroad stands on a siding by an enormous stack of wood bark in some Pennsylvania location. The card contains this note: "Bark is used in the Largest Tannery in the World."

Another commodity that moved by rail and was produced at trackside was salt. The works of the Pennsylvania Salt Manufacturing Company, part of the famous Michigan Salt Pool, at Wyandotte, Michigan, are shown in this World War I—era card.

Pennsylvania Salt Manufacturing Co.,
Wyandotte, Mich.

Slate, another bulk commodity, was sent by rail. A slate quarry near the northeastern Pennsylvania community of Slatington adjoins the rails of one of the four local railroads.

Part of the railroad corridor are these carbon-copy dwellings for mill workers and their families in Red Stone, New Hampshire. A substantial wooden fence separates the company housing from the White Mountain line of the Maine Central Railroad.

Ohio's extensive brick and tile manufacturers, the "mud industry," annually shipped thousands of cars of their finished products. The Richwood Clay Company, situated on the Dayton branch of the Erie Railroad, depended wholly on rail transport.

The nation's cattle and sheep industries were important seasonal shippers for midwestern and western carriers. The Union Pacific Railroad switched these stockyards at Valley, Nebraska, near the South Omaha meat-packing district.

A Daily Scene at Stock Yards at Valley, Nebr.   Mons Johnson, Publisher

Numerous railroads, including the Union Pacific Railroad, required huge amounts of block ice to prevent spoilage of fresh fruit and vegetable shipments. The "Largest Ice House in the West" adjoins Union Pacific tracks at Evanston, Wyoming.

The Largest Ice Houses in the West, at Evanston, Wyo. 11.

Before motor carriers captured the business, railroads annually handled enormous quantities of poultry and eggs. This trackside shipper, W. B. Barefoot & Co., sent processed poultry and eggs from its railroad corridor site in Cowan, Indiana. The Lake Erie & Western, part of the New York Central system, served the plant.

An important regional coal hauler, the Norfolk & Western Railway also vigorously promoted agricultural development along its lines in Ohio, Virginia, and West Virginia. The company's farm near Ivor, Virginia, functioned as an agricultural experiment station.

NORFOLK & WESTERN RAILWAY FARM, IVOR, VA.

Grain elevators are ubiquitous along rail lines in the Midwest and Great Plains. Farmers with their wagons loaded with corn gather at the Peter Hatterscheid elevator alongside the Minneapolis & St. Louis Railroad in Corwith, Iowa, on January 3, 1913.

Grain elevators largely overshadow the two-story Minneapolis & St. Louis Railroad depot at Clarksfield, Minnesota. And they are the principal architectural features in Dorchester, Nebraska, on the Chicago, Burlington & Quincy Railroad's mainline across the state.

Depot and Elevators, Clarkfield, Minn.

46-K   Grain Elevators   Dorchester, Neb

While depot hotels continued to serve patrons during the early twentieth century, it was more common to have public sleeping facilities near the station. Both hotels and boardinghouses were part of the railroad corridor. Two hotels abut the station grounds of the Chicago, Burlington & Quincy Railroad in Villisca, Iowa.

One of the country's loveliest hotels was the Mount Pleasant Hotel at the base of Mount Washington, northwest of North Conway, New Hampshire. The Mountain division of the Maine Central Railroad passed by the hotel's main entrance.

The Mt. Pleasant Hotel-Bretton Woods White Mountains, N. H.

8065 Copyrighted 1910 by N. Weston Pease North Conway N. H.

Since railroad builders sought the lowest grades and also served communities started along waterways, streams frequently shared the railroad corridor. That was fine as long as the waters remained within their banks. Kansas City, Kansas, and Kansas City, Missouri, felt the ravages of the flooding Kansas (Kaw) and Missouri Rivers in June 1908. An area photographer took a series of flood-related pictures that were then converted into a set of postcard views, including one of the Chicago Great Western's inundated freight house.

Kansas City Flood, June, 1908.—Freight Yard, Kansas City, Kan., in Background.

Kansas City Flood, June, 1908.—West Bottoms Street Scene, Near Depot.

PEOPLE

AND

RAILROADS

At times onlookers at a wreck site might pitch in to help. In this view card, sheep are being rescued from several slat-sided stockcars after a mishap at an unknown location in 1912.

Train wrecks regularly drew crowds of spectators. Makers of real-photo cards seized the opportunity to capitalize on these unfortunate yet dramatic events. The public often expected such souvenirs.

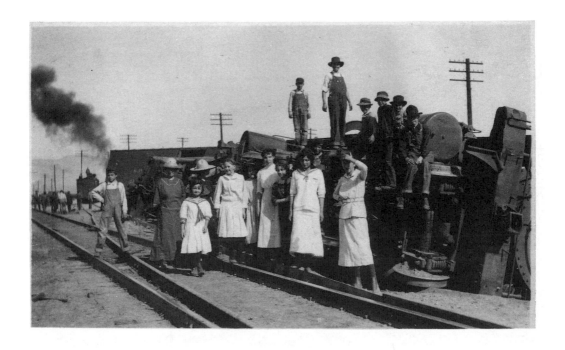

A couple is apparently waiting to leave an Oregon Short Line station. A person's "Sunday best" was the usual dress for a railroad journey. This real-photo card is marked: "Sunday April 25th—1909, O.S.L. Depot." This view, perhaps taken by a Kodak postcard camera, was likely a one-of-a-kind image.

A group relaxes in a whimsical pose on board a typical chair car of the turn of the century.

Signed "The Trio," three young women stand on the tracks, likely in Monmouth, Illinois, in March 1911.

High water drew a group of young adults to an

Omaha Road bridge near Henderson, Minnesota, on May 3, 1912.

A couple poses on board a baggage car about 1910. The commentary on the reverse side reads: "This was taken in the baggage car on the ping pong [probably a pet name for a local passenger train] last summer when I was up to Montpelier. We look sick, don't we?"

Members of a passenger train crew were in a cheery mood when a real-photo card was made of them at an unidentified time and place.

Commercial photographers found it profitable to make images of customers aboard fake rear observation platforms. This phenomenon was a popular part of the picture postcard craze.

The Electric Studio in Salt Lake City, Utah, photographed Oregon Short Line employees who were also officers of either the Brotherhood of Railroad Trainmen or the Order of Railway Conductors, two railroad operating unions.

A commercial photographer catches a family "leaving"
Denver, Colorado, on an imaginary Union Pacific "limited" train.

A nautical motif is employed by a photographer to promote Savanna, Illinois, a railroad division point on the east bank of the Mississippi River. An image of the local Chicago, Milwaukee & St. Paul depot is superimposed on the pilot wheel.

Army recruits march to a waiting train of the Denver & Rio

Grande Railroad at Fort Logan, Colorado, near Denver, during World War I.

91485 - RECRUITS ENTRAINING DENVER & RIO GRANDE R.R. FORT LOGAN, COLO.

Troops might be part of the commotion at trackside. Baggage is being unloaded at a New York Central Railroad siding in Pine Camp, New York (later Camp Drum), near Watertown, in 1911. And troops are detraining from Michigan Central Railroad coaches at Battle Creek, Michigan, during the Great War.

THE TEAMS AND BAGGAGE WAGONS, AT THE TRAIN, PINE, CAMP, N.Y.

"Just Arrived"—Going to Camp Custer, Battle Creek, Mich.

Railroads and private organizations, businesses, and institutions operated countless excursion extras. Here visitors to a "Seed Corn Special" accommodate a photographer at the Chicago Great Western Railroad station in Reinbeck, Iowa, in 1912.

A group mostly of returning servicemen crowd a coach on a special Missouri, Kansas & Texas Railway train to the oil boomtown of Burkburnett, Texas, northwest of Wichita Falls, in 1919. The lure of sudden riches attracted hundreds of men.

An unidentified group of men pose from a gondola car attached to a work train on the Detroit & Mackinac Railway. The reference is to an unknown tragedy at Metz, Michigan.

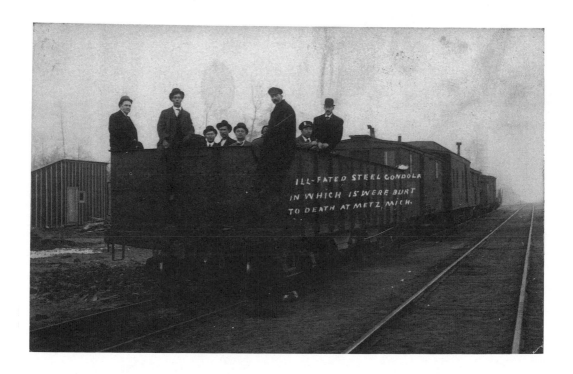

Part of working on the railroad involved initial line construction. Graders are shaping the right-of-way of the Wisconsin & Northern Railroad near Crandon, Wisconsin, in about 1909. This pike, which later joined the Chicago, Milwaukee & St. Paul Railway and then the Soo Line, is being built between Van Ostrand and Crandon, in the northeastern part of the Badger state.

The exact location of this construction scene, taken about 1914, in McKenzie County, North Dakota, is uncertain. Perhaps graders are preparing the Great Northern Railway extension from Fairview to Watford City or building a shortline that failed to survive.

Workers are moving earth and laying track at "North Bend," likely North Bend,
Washington, on the Milwaukee Road's fifty-five-mile Cedar Falls–Everett branch.

Maintenance-of-way workers take a break

from their backbreaking labors to satisfy a photographer.

Dated May 28, 1911, this real-photo card captures four track workers with their hand-pump section car.

A much larger assemblage of trackmen pose with their section cars in front of an unidentified combination depot.

A small-town station agent and a fellow employee or friend look into a camera lens in the office of the joint Northern Pacific Railway and Oregon Railroad & Navigation Company depot at Grangeville, Idaho, in 1911.

In a more candid shot, the agent at Elmwood Junction, New Hampshire, where two lines of the Boston & Maine Railroad cross, works at his telegraphic instruments. Most railroads before World War II required station personnel to wear uniforms or at least an official cap.

RR58 ELMWOOD JNCT. N.H. 1935

Little is known about this real-photo card, except that the subject is Clara Marie Swanson, who was twenty-two years old in 1910. She might be a depot agent, custodian, or telegrapher, jobs which women could hold in a male-dominated industry.

The crew of a "camel-back" locomotive takes a few minutes off to please a
photographer in the sprawling yards of the Erie Railroad at Susquehanna, Pennsylvania.

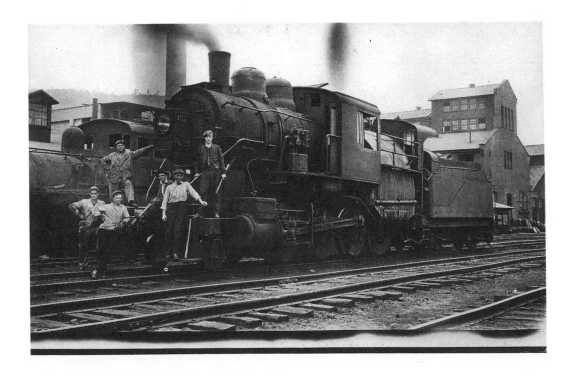

In Altoona, Pennsylvania, the great shops town on the Pennsylvania Railroad, thousands of families depended on the company payroll. The Wheel Shop was part of this massive repair complex.

EXTERIOR OF PENNSYLVANIA RAILROAD WHEEL SHOP, 12TH ST., ALTOONA, PA.

3616·PUBLISHED BY SILVERMAN BROS

Seemingly the entire roundhouse or shop force gathers

on the turntable and on a giant locomotive for this picture.

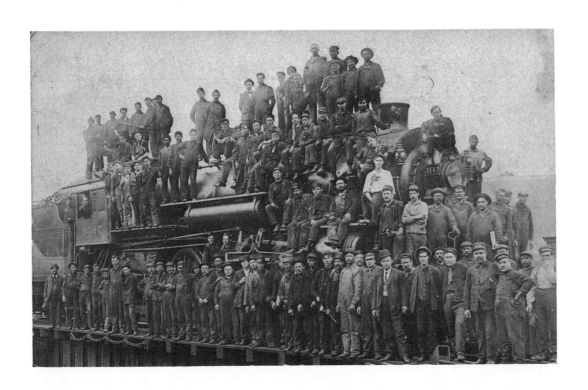

THE

LIGHTER SIDE

OF

RAILROADING

Boosters at Bonner, Montana, located on the transcontinental line

of the Northern Pacific Railway, show their "citron melons" with great pride.

Residents of Emporia, Kansas, suggest that

there were no town-country tensions in their community.

Our Farmers are Hard to "Beet"
At EMPORIA, KANS.

This novelty card was mailed from Madison Lake,

Minnesota, a village on the Chicago Great Western Railroad, in 1910.

Superimposed on a photograph of William Howard Taft, probably taken during the presidential campaign of 1908, are agricultural products that contribute to "Missouri prosperity."

The mythical Miss Phoebe Snow enjoys the scenery along the mainline of the Delaware, Lackawanna & Western Railroad. The card is an early view of Phoebe Snow and dates from before 1907.

View from the rear end of the Lackawanna Limited. The Daylight Flyer over the road of Anthracite.

Americans usually tolerated bums and hoboes, and the image of the wandering traveler who "rode the rods" was universally known and at times even admired.

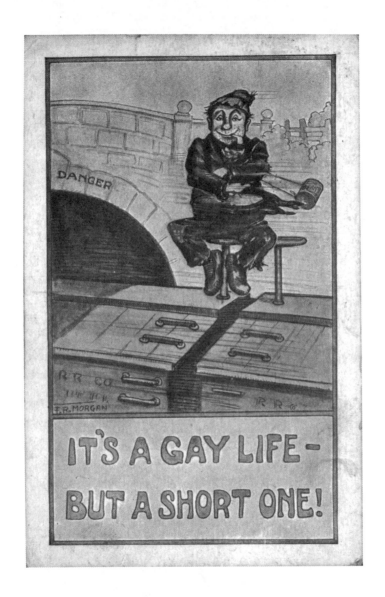

Rather than an artist's drawing, a photograph of a "bo" is used in this specialty card that suggests "The Simple Life."

The Simple Life.   (Copyright.)

While both happy and sad, a soldier embarking for the war in Europe might have sent this *"On to FRANCE" "Goodbye Girlie"* card, which the Chicago Daily News *issued.*

The dominance of the railroad in the nation's mail distribution system is obvious in this drawing.

HURRY THAT LETTER

I know You're busy,
No doubt time rushes by
unreckoned;
But still a card with just "Hello"
Would only take a second.

This card, whose sender "arrived safe" and
"went to the dance," was mailed from St. Paul, Minnesota.

"WE HAVE THE WHOLE CAR TO OURSELVES."

Americans' funny-bones were tickled during the picture postcard era with such captions as "This is the Crowd that Met Me at the Depot" and "We Don't Know Where We're Going, But We're On Our way."

This is the Crowd that Met Me at the Depot.

22   We Don't Know Where We're Going, But We're On Our Way.

Although individuals along the chain between sender and receiver might smile at a cover, they likely could not understand the personal message on this card. Some writers preferred code instead of prose.

A card sender in 1906 selected this humorous message and then made personal notations. The "Big 4" is a reference to the Cleveland, Cincinnati, Chicago & St. Louis Railway, popularly dubbed the Big Four. This New York Central affiliate served the four midwestern cities of its corporate name.

The railroad was the link between communities for most Americans. An artist for the Detroit Publishing Company captured the pathos that was frequently part of the departure of a passenger train.

14,007—Detroit Publishing Co.

MONDAY MORNING

COPYRIGHT, 1900, BY LIFE PUBLISHING CO.

I. M

INDEX